AF818231

# NO FLUFF SERIES

**LEARN ABOUT A TOPIC
IN UNDER 30 PAGES**

# HOW TO COMPILE BUSINESS REQUIREMENTS TO PREPARE FOR A SALESFORCE SALES CLOUD IMPLEMENTATION

**NO FLUFF PRESS**
PRINTED IN THE UNITED STATES OF AMERICA

How To Compile Business Requirements To
Prepare For A Salesforce Sales Cloud Implementation

Copyright © 2021 By No Fluff Series

All Rights Reserved.

No Fluff Series is a series of titles about various topics.
No part of this book may be reproduced, or stored in a retrieval system, or transmitted in any form or by any means, electronic, mechanical, photocopying, recording, or otherwise, without express written permission by the No Fluff Series. All rights reserved.

The information contained in this book is sold without warranty, either expressed or implied. The publisher, dealer nor distributor will be held liable for any damages caused or alleged to have been caused directly or indirectly by this E-book or paperback format. Software may be updated and some material included in this book may be obsolete as capabilities could be retired or new capabilities have been introduced. No Fluff Series has tried to provide trademark information about all companies and products mentioned in this book by the appropriate use of Capitals, but No Fluff Series cannot guarantee the accuracy of this information.

ISBN-13: 978-1-955559-00-3
ISBN-10: 1-955559-00-7

Printed in the United States of America

First Printing, 2021

No Fluff Press
U.S.A.
www.nofluffseries.com

# Introduction

IF YOU WANT TO LEARN MORE about Salesforce or the company you work for either recently purchased or has had Salesforce for a while, then this book is for you! Regardless if you are in Sales, Marketing, IT or any department within your company, this book is ideal for anyone wanting to know where to start in compiling your company's Salesforce business requirements. This book is also beneficial if your Salesforce is already customized, and you need to know where to start in understanding the best way to compile requirements to make various changes or recommendations.

Salesforce is such a large system with so many great capabilities and you may seem overwhelmed that you were daunted with this task, especially if you have never seen Salesforce before and may have only heard about the system in your past experience. Fear no more, as this book is the first step in making sure you are compiling the necessary business requirements prior to implementing any customizations by understanding what is in place and how things may need to change. Compiling your company's business requirements is part of the overall implementation process that no one really talks about, but is truly one of the most important aspects of actually implementing Salesforce. Rest assured, you will be looking, sounding and feeling like a true Salesforce rock star if you follow these steps within your scoping calls when compiling each department's business requirements within this short book!

# Step 1: Understanding Salesforce Terminology

BEFORE HAVING MEETINGS WITH VARIOUS departments to compile their business requirements, you must first learn Salesforce Terminology. This way, throughout various meetings, you start to use these terms and explain what they mean to your fellow colleagues, so everyone is speaking the same language. In essence, you will be educating your audience from the start, so when there are change requests or other discussions taking place, your colleagues can reference the items by their correct names, and you can quickly identify what they are talking about to continue discussing their needs. This may seem unrealistic, or you may be thinking that you work with people that are stuck in their ways, but if you start from the beginning of your work tenure or from the start of when the company has purchased/reviewing Salesforce, it truly comes down to setting the precedence with correct Salesforce Terminology.

## GENERAL TERMS

- **Salesforce Instance or Salesforce Org:** Both these words mean the same thing. This is the Salesforce system that you and your team login to each day. That's it! It seems more sophisticated than it needs to be. These words are used interchangeably depending on whom you speak with (i.e., your Salesforce Rep, other Salesforce Users, other Salesforce Admins, help documents, etc.) but they mean the same thing.
- **Lightning or Classic:** These two words will come up depending on if you are working for a company that has had Salesforce for a while. Lightning is the newest Salesforce User Interface aka "look and feel" of Salesforce itself. Classic is the older Salesforce User Interface. If your company just purchased Salesforce, then you will be defaulted to Lightning automatically and will only work within Lightning. If your company has had Salesforce for a while, then they still may be using Classic and may eventually need to migrate (switch over) to Lightning.
- **Edition of Salesforce Sales Cloud:** This is the version of Salesforce Sales Cloud your company purchased. Examples of editions include Essentials, Professional, Enterprise or Unlimited Edition. Each edition has varying capabilities

in the order that the editions were written. Therefore, it is important to know which edition of Salesforce you are using, as some of the capabilities discussed in this book may not be available or is limited within the edition your company has purchased.

- **Production:** The live version of Salesforce that you and your team use every day.
- **Sandbox:** Where you and your developers can create custom code and/or conduct testing for various additional customizations. A sandbox is where you can explore and test various items prior to pushing or deploying these customizations into Production, which could affect your users and other functionality and you want to make sure all is working accordingly.
- **Business to Business (B-to-B) and/or Business to Consumer (B-to-C) Selling:** Salesforce out-of-the-box is defaulted for businesses that sell 'business to business' with the use of contact records associated to account records. If you are a business that sells only 'business to consumer', or needs the ability to sell both 'business to business' and 'business to consumer'; then this feature is called, "Person Accounts" ('business to consumer' selling within Salesforce) and you can request this feature to be enabled.

## SALESFORCE EVERYDAY USER TERMS

- **Fields:** These are data points that are displayed on an Object. Examples may include: Name, Company, Phone, Mobile, Email, etc. Fields are information that users will populate as they are creating or updating a record. Fields that come out-of-the-box with Salesforce are called "Standard" fields, while the custom ones you create are called "Custom" fields. Every field has a 'Field Type', meaning the field could be a 'Free Text' field, a 'Picklist' field, a 'Date' field and other options.
- **Related Lists:** This is a list of records for each specific Object(s) that are associated to the record you are viewing. For example, if you are on a specific Account record, let's say "Testing Center 123", then a related list to this Account that is shown could be the Contact Object with the actual contact records listed that work at that Account. Simply put, Related Lists just display information by Object and lists the specific records within those Objects, for easy reference of related items to the actual record you are viewing.
- **Page Layouts:** This is where fields are positioned on the page. You are able to create named sections for users to easily reference fields that are applicable to that section. You can also determine which related objects (aka 'Related Lists') that are displayed on each Page Layout to display related information.
- **Record Types:** Allow you to control only relevant information to be displayed per the Record Type. For example, on the Account Object, a company may want to create Record Types for their 'retail' accounts and their 'wholesale' accounts.

This way, you get to choose which fields and related lists are displayed for the retail accounts, which may differ from the fields and related lists you want displayed on the wholesale accounts.

- **Buttons:** Examples of Buttons are the following, "Edit", "Clone", "Delete" and other buttons that are standard or custom built. These are items users click on that then allow the user to do something and/or can run an automation.
- **Objects:** Anything you can create a record on, is an Object. A "Lead" is an Object, an "Account" is an Object, a "Contact" is an Object, and many others. This term will be utilized constantly by everyone. Objects that come out-of-the box when you purchase Salesforce are called "Standard" Objects, while Objects you create that are unique to your company are called "Custom" Objects.
- **Tabs:** Are the Objects with a Tab you can click on for ease of access. Tabs can be displayed across the top of your screen when you login to Salesforce, or can be seen if you click to see all tab options that you have access to. Again, these are Objects that can be accessed quickly by clicking on their corresponding Tab.
- **Activity:** These are all the communications that have taken place on a record, such as emails, follow up tasks or calls made. Activities can either be a "Task" or an "Event" Record.
- **Chatter:** This feature is very similar to social media capabilities, except this is fully tracked on a per record basis, or a per user basis or through "Groups" of users or a mixture or all these items. Chatter allows users to post questions, provide answers, tag people to alert them and many other features to collaborate and communicate with each other.
- **List Views:** These have preset criteria that you create for users and/or users can create on their own to easily manage their records. List Views can be used to sort records, update fields within the list (with a few exceptions), run an automation by clicking a button on top of the List View or even can click on a record to see the full details. An example of a List View is for a sales person to select an "Active Leads" List View, to then quickly display those specific records that fit that criteria in a list format. A number of List Views can be created and for any Object that has a Tab associated to it.
- **Approval Process:** This is a process you build within Salesforce to allow users to submit a record to be reviewed (most likely sent to their manager) that then determines what happens next. Possible outcomes could be an approval, or a rejection with a recommendation of what needs to be changed or updated. Approval Processes are common on the Quote Object to gain manager approval, prior to allowing a user to send a proposal to a prospect/customer.

## LEVEL OF ACCESS TERMS

- **Users:** These are the people that have or had access to your Salesforce. Users are the personnel that will be working within your Salesforce.
- **Profiles:** Typically created by department (or by department subsets) and assigned to each user that permits the relevant security access to items within your Salesforce. There are a few layers of security and level of access that can be permitted to users, as will be discussed in this terminology section. Just know, Profiles are required to be assigned to each user and is a great starting point to get an idea of which users have access to various items within your Salesforce.
- **Roles:** This reflects the Hierarchy of Users within your Company. It is important this is set up correctly as Roles have an effect on the potential access of other Role Records and for Team Reporting, as this hierarchy can be referenced when building Reports/Dashboards in Salesforce.
- **Permission Sets:** Can be a 'one-off' additional permission or multiple additional permissions that can be granted to a specific user(s). Remember, Profiles are the high-level starting point and have to be assigned per user. Permissions simply grant specific user(s) you assign them to, to then be able to have access or be able to do something that others with the same Profile do not have access to.
- **Sharing Sets:** Sharing Settings are global across the entire system and list each Object that you can decide if you would like to make each Object's Records Public with various options, such as Read/Write/Transfer or be set to Private. This just specifies if you would like to have users be able to access other users' records that they do not own, and also create exceptions of records that may need to be globally accessible with specific criteria by Object.

## CUSTOM CODE TERMS

- **Apex:** The custom code that can be added into Salesforce to further automate or run various processes. Apex is broken out by 'Classes' and 'Triggers'.
- **Visualforce:** A custom-coded page that can be created to combine a number of data fields, records and objects that are built to your company's business requirements. A Visualforce Page is an advanced feature to be used as part of an existing Page Layout for an Object or can be its own Tab and full page to then run an automation or for viewing information in a specific format. Visualforce Pages can also be used as a public page, such as an extension of your website. Simply put, it is a custom page built through custom code that can be used in a variety of ways to display information, capture information and/or run automations.

## AUTOMATION TERMS

- **Workflows:** This can be accomplished without any code and allows you to determine specific criteria to be able to either update another field, create a Task and/or send an email to an internal user or external person. This is an easy way to take care of many simple automation needs through point-and-click capabilities.
- **Validation Rules:** Allows you to write formula syntax code to ensure users are populating fields correctly or not able to proceed without having a combination of fields populated. Based on a user's action or inaction, then lets the user know what they need to correct before being able to proceed or save the record.
- **Process Builder:** A number of If/Then statements, and also includes nearly all Workflow capabilities, that allows you to automate various processes without any coding. There are limitations to Process Builder compared to Flows and Apex Custom Code.
- **Flows:** This is a more advanced point-and-click feature that provides a variety of automation capabilities. Flows can allow users to be guided in a screen to do a step-by-step process or run an automation (or both). The guided step-by-step process works on how the user populates fields displayed on the page, which then determines the next screen that is displayed to provide guidance based on specific answers. Flows can also be used to run automatically or based on an action by a user that triggers the Flow, to do various automation items. As of now, Workflow and Process Builder capabilities appear to be transitioning and replicated within the Flow feature. Keep in mind, the Flow feature is the future of point-and-click automation within Salesforce, and could potentially replace Workflows and Process Builder capabilities.

# Step 2: Who Should Take Part in "Business Requirement" Meetings

WHO YOU DECIDE TO INCLUDE in your business requirement meetings will drastically have an effect on the results of the compiled system requirements. If the personnel chosen to be included in the meetings have no interest in implementing Salesforce, or really do not know the processes of their department, then most likely the requirements you compile will not be relevant and your Salesforce Implementation final product may not turn out as your company had desired.

Do not make the mistake of failing from the start because the personnel chosen to be the main contributors are not able to communicate what they need from an implementation. Setting these expectations when discussing who to include within your business requirement meetings is a critical juncture in proceeding with the remainder of this book. The following is a list of items that will help you vet the types of people you should and should not include in your business requirements meetings.

- **Turn the Organization Hierarchy Upside Down:** Everyone knows who the top dogs are at their own companies and everyone always wants to be in their good graces in order to keep their job. Everyone at the company also knows where they stand in the overall Organization Hierarchy, which may be near the bottom, middle or top region. But when it comes to compiling business requirements, these bottom and near bottom personnel are the high value add when it comes to compiling all the critical details to have a successful Salesforce Implementation. Yes, the executives and department heads are the ones in control and are providing the funding for this project, but these executives and department heads are not the 'Foot Soldiers' that are gathering and collecting information that is critical for your Salesforce to be valuable. In essence, executives and department heads have an understanding of processes, but may not know all the refined details, and that is why turning the organization hierarchy upside down makes these 'Foot Soldiers' so valuable. They are to be included in these meetings to discuss all the questions they ask customers/prospects, data points needed to complete various steps and any other details that are field-specific items that you need to document. This does not mean that you disregard nor exclude executives or department heads, but what this does mean is that you need to include personnel at all organizational levels, specifically 'Foot Soldiers' who speak with customers/prospects regularly and know the details of the day-to-day items to be part of your meetings.

- **Include people with years of experience at the company or who know the processes:** Including personnel that is very familiar with the internal company processes is extremely helpful as a starting point to compile the necessary business requirements. They are able to detail the specifics in regards to the information collected or needing to be collected and discuss which people are involved through various parts of the process that may include a number of internal personnel. This allows you to map out the step-by-step process by gaining this detailed insight. In addition, people with years of experience at the company can provide context of what was the process prior and why the current process has evolved to what it is today. Overall, this is a great start for you to have a clear understanding of what is currently happening at the company through various departments, for you to then replicate within Salesforce. Please note, this does not mean that you cannot improve or question current processes to make them more efficient, especially now that you are utilizing a CRM system to assist in streamlining various processes. This is why including personnel that are knowledgeable about the current day-to-day, allows you to then provide recommendations to further improve company operations systematically after seeing the full picture.
- **Department Specific:** Yes, Salesforce can literally be the focal point or simply have an impact on a number of departments, even if it is not being utilized as the core system of that department at your company. But this does not mean that you include everyone in every meeting or have every department included in meetings designated for only a specific department that you are trying to compile their specific business requirements. This could create an environment that is more hostile and argumentative, versus being productive and having personnel provide valuable insight by contributing ideas and knowledge about existing processes. This does not mean that you only include only the department you are focused on, but instead, may want to include at least one other person from a department that certain business requirements may overlap. For example, let's say you have a meeting scheduled with your Sales Department and the meeting is to discuss the Lead Object and the Lead Management process. It may be beneficial to also include one other individual from the Marketing Department since they have an effect on delivering Leads and would be great for them to add their insight and also understand the Sales Department's processes of managing Lead records. This way, everyone is aligned and knows relatively what each other is contributing to the process. You know your company best and having department-specific meetings is a great way to optimize everyone's time in compiling business requirements. It also allows personnel to contribute

and collaborate with one another to provide additional 'value-add', that could improve creating more efficient and effective processes within your Salesforce.

- **Limit the Number of People:** The types of people are just as important as the number of people you choose to include within your business requirement meetings. Having too many company personnel may become unproductive by having numerous conflicting opinions that may lead to arguments, or removing a number of personnel from their day-to-day items and consuming their time that may be better utilized elsewhere. And having too few personnel may not allow you to get all the information necessary to truly build out the business requirements that fulfill the departmental needs. It typically is ideal to include at least one person at each level of that department to be sure to capture business requirements from the lowest level to the upper management; so all party's requirements are fulfilled. It would also be ideal for these personnel at each level to be knowledgeable about the current processes and potentially be with the company for a number of years. Lastly, based on the business requirement meeting you are having, ask yourself, if the meeting that is planned for one department indirectly or directly affects another department? If so, it would be advantageous, but not required, to include at least one person from that other department(s). Again, these other personnel from a department other than whom is the focal point may add value to the discussions taking place, or at least be aligned with their counterpart department by becoming familiar with their processes to potentially improve their own.

**Helpful Hint:** This whole book is about compiling your company business requirements to prepare for an Implementation, and whom you include in meetings to compile those requirements could ultimately have an effect on the outcome of the implementation itself.

# Step 3: Identify Standard Objects You Will Utilize

NOW THAT YOU KNOW WHOM to include in various business requirement meetings, next is to determine which Standard Objects that are applicable to your company. Not every company will utilize all the Standard Objects that come out-of-the-box with Salesforce, and that is okay and very common! There are a number of Objects that come with Salesforce, and it is typically best to review and identify which Standard Objects are applicable to you and your company as the first step. The most commonly used Objects by companies are the Leads, Accounts, Contacts, Opportunities, Quotes, Products, Prices Books, Activities (Task & Events) and Campaigns, which are the basics. Again, that does not mean you have to use all these Standard Objects nor other Standard Objects not listed here. Some Standard Objects that are not necessarily as commonly used, such as Assets, which tracks a specific piece of equipment/asset that has been installed or leased to a customer that can also store other information. This Standard Object may not be relevant to you and your business and therefore, most likely will be hidden so users do not see items that they will not use.

**Helpful Hint:** It is always best to try to use Standard Objects prior to thinking about or creating Custom Objects. This affects the following items:

1. **Standard Functionality:** Certain processes work best using Standard Objects and is the reason why Salesforce provides them out-of-the-box. An example of this is the 'Lead Conversion Process' which is when a user converts a Lead Record to start working on an Opportunity Record (a sales deal). This conversion process comes out-of-the-box, instead of you having to create something custom. Every company has different business requirements, and it does not mean that creating a custom Lead Conversion process is a 'bad thing', it is just best to utilize standard functionality as much as possible and build custom items when it is truly necessary.
2. **Easier to Scale:** You are able to purchase pre-developed Apps on Salesforce's AppExchange. The majority of these Apps can be customized, and they typically work very well because they are built to reference Standard Objects. Again, most Apps still work with the use of Custom Objects, but it most likely will take additional customizations that you or

your developer will need to configure to make it work. This is also true for pre-built integrations that may need additional configuration with the use of Custom Objects over Standard Objects.

# Step 4: Compiling Field Requirements For A Standard Object

IF YOU HAVE NOT CHOSEN every Standard Object that will be utilized for your company as of now, do not worry, as you can follow this same process for every Object that you would like to conduct a review with you and your team. At this point of the book, you are now ready to start compiling your business requirements for each applicable department within your organization by starting off with Field Requirements for each applicable Standard Object. Take each Standard Object one at a time. If you skip ahead to other Objects or discuss multiple objects at once, it may cause confusion for all parties. Even if someone in your meeting is trying to discuss, as an example, the Opportunity Object, when you are still on the Account Object; you should document what they have said and bring everyone back to the Account Object. This way, you continue to complete the business requirements on the current Object you are on, prior to moving forward. Of course, you still have noted the comment made, so when the meeting about the Opportunity Object takes place, you will be sure to circle back to the item that was brought up prior.

**Helpful Hint #1:** This does not mean you will capture everything for that Object all in one meeting. Sometimes when you move on to the next Object, some of your team members may come up with other fields that were not discussed on prior Objects. These new ideas that are suggested, due to various discussions taking place that may not have been brought up prior, may prove to be valuable and eventually included in the final implementation.

**Helpful Hint #2:** This is a fluid process, be open and be considerate of others. And most importantly, continue to listen to everyone's feedback as you make progress through all of your various business requirement meetings.

**Recommended Steps to Compile Fields for a Standard Object:** Regardless of which Standard Object you are discussing in your meeting, it should follow a similar process as described below:

a. **Review Standard Fields (also known as the out-of-the-box fields) that come with Salesforce first.** Just like Standard Objects, always try to use what comes with Salesforce prior to creating something custom. In this case, there are Standard Fields that come with Salesforce for every Standard Object. Discuss each field and determine which ones are applicable and which ones can be removed from the Page Layout.

b. **Are any of the Standard Fields you decided to keep needing to be customized?** Out of the standard fields you decided are valuable to your company and want to use, do any of those fields need to be updated to be even more relevant? An example of this is a field called "Industry" (a picklist field – drop down set of values a user can select one option from). These set picklist values for this field that comes out-of-the-box when you first purchase Salesforce may not be the values you would like to utilize internally. Therefore, you can customize these options by adding, removing and updating values to what you and the team have decided to have as "Industry" classifications. Picklist fields and naming conventions of how the field name appears of actual Standard Fields, are items that you can change to make the system relevant to you and your company.

c. **For some Standard Objects, there are hidden fields that are not on the Page Layout nor are they visible to you and your users**. It is important to go into the back end of your Salesforce and review all the fields that exist on the Standard Object you are discussing. Certain fields out-of-the-box are hidden and when you go in the back end of your Salesforce, you will be able to see all the fields that are available to review. You can then determine if any of the hidden fields need to be made unhidden because they are useful to your company.

d. **Then discuss the custom fields that are needed per Object.** This is an open discussion, and it is important that you constantly keep asking your personnel questions to get more and more information from them. Be sure that you become the moderator. A great way to get everyone involved in the discussion is to role play what happens for each applicable Object you are discussing. This will assist in getting everyone to start thinking in a process-oriented manner and walks you through the current process, for everyone to contribute and provide their ideas. When compiling the custom fields that are relevant to the Object that is being discussed, it is critical to identify what "Type" of field is best to capture the information you want users to be able to populate.

   i. **When you identify a new custom field, ask yourself, "What type of field should this be?"** Meaning, should this be a free text, a picklist field, a date field or something else? How you determine the answer to this question is very easy and most people overcomplicate it.

   ii. **Picklist:** If you want users to select an answer from your pre-defined choices, you will use a Picklist field. Picklist fields are most optimal for reporting due to the consistency of set values! You do also have the choice of a 'Multi-Select' Picklist field, which is the same as a Picklist field with pre-set values that you create, except the user is able to select multiple options if they wish. The downside to a Multi-Select Picklist field is that it is one of the worst fields for reporting purposes if you want consistent reporting per value that is selectable. Try to stay away from Multi-Select picklist fields if the field is critical for reporting purposes. Otherwise, it is a great field type to select a number of options in a single field with pre-set values that you created for your users to select from.

iii. **Free Text:** If the field needs flexibility and will have variable information, then a free text field that is either Text, Text Area, Text (Long) are the best options. These different types of Free Text options are not complicated, as the only difference between the three types is as follows: Text has up to 255 character limit and all on one singular line (meaning the user is not able to press enter to skip down a line), while the Text Area is the same character limit of up to 255, but it permits the user to skip down a line as long as the text is within the character limit. Lastly, Text (Long) is up to a 131,072 character limit and allows the User to skip multiple lines, very similar to a free form field.

iv. **Date or Date/Time:** If there is a date that needs to be captured then the field will be a Date field. If both a date and time need to be captured, then a Date/Time Field would be ideal.

v. **Number:** Any numerical value.

vi. **Currency:** Any numerical value that is a currency value.

vii. **Checkbox:** A simple checkbox field. A word of caution: in some cases, a Picklist field with a Yes or a No option, is more ideal than a Checkbox field. This is because a blank value can be defaulted that then requires the user to update the field to a Yes or No value. This way, the User has to choose an option. As an example, you really do not know if the User meant to leave this field unchecked on purpose, or if they forgot to checkbox the field. Granted, there are Salesforce features that can be implemented to confirm this, but the Yes/No Picklist option is sometimes a better option than a checkbox as you can require the user to choose a Yes or a No answer. It truly comes down to the use case of needing a checkbox field versus a designation through a picklist field that can provide the option to force a user to select an actual option.

viii. **Lookup:** To simplify this, a lookup allows a user to search for an existing record to associate with another record. The Object designation of this field determines which records appear for that Object that can be searchable and then selected. In essence, a Lookup field could allow a user to associate a record that exists on a different Object from the record you are associating it to; or could be referencing another record from the same Object. For example, if the field called "Lead Source" was populated with a picklist value called 'Customer Referral', you may want to track the specific Customer Account that actually provided the referral. This way you can pull a report and send them a gift card, thanking them for sending the referral. To accomplish this, you would create a Lookup field on the Lead Object, but designating or looking up to the Account Object. When a User updates this field on their Lead record, they can search for existing Customer Account records. Then they can select the specific Account record that provided the Lead Referral, to associate that Account record with the Lead record you are currently working on.

ix. **Master Detail Lookup:** This is the exact same as the Lookup field type above, with additional capabilities. First, this field systematically will always be required to be populated when creating a new record, and this cannot be changed. This is because the Master Detail Lookup field type is saying: in order to create this record, it is required to be associated to another record every single time. Another capability when using a Master Detail Lookup is the ability to create other custom fields that utilize the 'Rollup Summary' field type. This allows you to reference records from a related Object that is associated with the current record you are on. You are then able to calculate a record 'Count' or a 'SUM' value based off of related records (there are other calculations that can be done as well). Simply put, a Master Detail Lookup allows you to associate a record, is always a required field and provides the availability for a user to create calculated Rollup fields.

x. **Formula:** Allows you to create a calculation, build logic for an outcome (like an If/Then statement), or pull a field value from a related record to be displayed in 'Read Only' format. Pulling a field value from a related record that is displayed on the current record, allows the user to not have to go back and forth between related records for a field (or a combination of a few fields) to be displayed for them to reference on the current record. Formula fields require formula syntax writing capabilities, but are very useful fields that at some point, will most likely be utilized within your Salesforce.

xi. **Other Fields:** There are other Field Types you can choose from, but those mentioned above are the most commonly used and fulfill the majority of what you are trying to accomplish when documenting and compiling your company business requirements.

Let's walk through an example of the Lead Object so you can see how the compiling business requirements process works in a step-by-step process.

# Step 5: Example Of Compiling Field Requirements For A Standard Object

WHETHER YOU JUST BOUGHT SALESFORCE Sales Cloud or are reviewing an existing Salesforce instance, a potential starting Standard Object is likely to be the Lead Object. As a reminder, the first step is to review the 'Standard Fields' that come with Salesforce. This way, you can maximize and determine what is applicable and not applicable that comes standard within the system. This is easier when you start off with a new Salesforce Instance, but you can absolutely still review these Standard Fields within an existing Salesforce, as they may or may not be valid any longer, or need to be further customized to become more relevant. Either way, this is a fairly easy process that is highly recommended to ensure you are maximizing each Standard field as explained below.

**Standard Fields you should MOST LIKELY KEEP and usually DO NOT NEED to make changes to:**

**Lead Owner** – is the user who is assigned as the Owner of that record.

**Name** – this is displayed as one unified field, but when you edit the record, there are multiple fields, such as Salutation (Mr., Ms., Mrs., etc.), First Name, Middle Name, Last Name and Suffix. Salutation is a Picklist field, which means there are set values that a User can choose from, but can only select one of the values. You are able to add, remove or edit available picklist options. The other Fields mentioned are Free Text fields, so your Users are able to input any name variation they choose, which makes sense as we all have different names.

**Company** – where users input the company name the Lead is employed.

**Title** – the position the Lead record holds at the company.

**Phone, Mobile, Email** – the Lead's contact information, each has their own separate field.

**Website** – this is where you input the company website.

**Address** – this is displayed as one unified field but when you edit the record, there are multiple fields, such as Street, City, State, Country and Zip Code. Out-of-the-box for the State and Country fields are Free Text, but it may be best to convert these fields into Picklist Options through Salesforce standard functionality, to ensure users do not have different variations using State acronyms or the infamous misspellings of items. This is also ideal for lead assignment rules or for marketing segmentation purposes to have State and Country values set as picklist values to easily filter through with a simple "equals to" versus the random "contains" value criteria that most likely will not provide all the results you are looking for.

**Standard Fields you should MOST LIKELY KEEP and usually NEED to make changes to:**

**Lead Source** – This field is how your prospects/customers find you and how you and your personnel find prospects/customers. This is an important field to keep track of what Sales/Marketing sources are generating new Leads and how many turn into potential Opportunities, aka sales deals! The picklist options need to be updated and tailored to your company avenues for generating Leads. Document all the sources and see which overlap, to make a concise list of clearly defined picklist options.

**Industry** – This field is the industry classification that the company is considered to be designated. Out-of-the-box values will most likely need to be customized to make the Picklist options relevant to your organization on how you classify the industry in which a company would be designated within your company. Only have relevant Industry options that are applicable to your type of business and that you believe are valuable. Do not keep options to have a variety, as they will not be used nor are relevant to your company.

**Lead Status** – This is one of the most important fields on the Lead Object, as it provides a high level overview of your company's "Lead Management" process and what is happening with each Lead Record.

*The following are questions you should ask your sales team to identify what Picklist options need to be available here, and in which order those picklist values will be set, as this will represent your company's "Lead Management" process:*

- When a Lead is initially created, what is the very first Lead Status of the Lead? Most common defaulted option is either "Open" or "New". Again, you can choose any name you wish for the first defaulted value. Keep in mind you should create something that is clear and specific to let everyone know that this is a brand new lead.
- Now that a new Lead record has been created and the salesperson tries to contact them; what is the status of the Lead now? Some companies like to keep it simple and have "Contacted" or "Working" as the status, regardless if the sales person connected with the actual Lead, as this will be documented within the "Activities" section of what took place. Other companies like the Lead Status to be very

specific, such as "Attempted to Contact" for an initial non-connected attempt. When the sales rep connects with the actual Lead, they would then update the Lead Status to something like "Contacted". The choice is yours based on your internal discussions, but do not get too granular such as "First call", "First call and first email", etc., as this is way too much for your sales person to keep track of and update (especially without any automation). Keep it simple yet effective – that is the goal!

- Now that you are communicating with the Lead, another picklist option recommended is a status of something like "On Hold". This is when the Lead wants to do business with you or wants to learn more about your products/services, but it is currently not the right time and to follow up with the Lead in a specified time period. You do not want your user to simply Unqualify the Lead, because the Lead is still possibly interested, and you do not want your user to Qualify the Lead because we do not know if they are wanting to proceed down your sales process just yet. Therefore, a status like "On Hold" is a great way to fulfill the requirement of someone interested and a follow up is scheduled to check in and continue working the Lead record. Of course, once the Lead is re-engaged, the user can simply update the Lead Status back to another status to show where this specific Lead Record is within the "Lead Management" process.
- Lastly, your final options are for the Lead to be "Unqualified" or "Qualified". "Unqualified" is that the Lead is not interested in what you are offering. Qualified will be auto-defaulted when the User converts the Lead by clicking the Convert Button. Converting means that the Lead is qualified and ready to create an Account Record, a Contact Record and an Opportunity Record (sales deal) for the user to start the Opportunity Sales Cycle. All you need to know is that Qualified means the record is no longer a Lead, and the user has now created a sales deal to progress through the Sales Cycle.

**Helpful Hint:** This Lead Status field is a critical field on the Lead Object. It is important to keep this field as concise and straight forward as possible, so your users are not confused on what to classify and understand each step of the "Lead Management" process.

**Standard Fields that are OPTIONAL because they may not be applicable to your company:**

**No. of Employees** – this is a field where users can input the size of the company. To be honest, this field is optional because if you are not using a data appending service to actually get this information or if this is not relevant in determining the Lead's potential fit to purchase your products/services; then this field is recommended to be removed from the Page layout.

**Rating** – this allows users to set a Rating if the Lead is Cold, Warm or Hot as the standard picklist options. Of course, you can customize these picklist options to display what your company's preference is, but this may be redundant for most companies as the Lead Status field should determine where the Lead is at in the "Lead Management" process. Some companies want a second classification to help prioritize Leads. Just know, this field typically gets updated once and then may never get updated again, which does not provide any valuable insight (unless automation is added or your users are diligent in updating this field).

**Helpful Hint:** The majority of any standard or custom fields can be removed off the Page Layout if they are not applicable to your business. There are very few exceptions of standard fields that are not able to be removed from the Page Layout, due to the system requiring that they stay on the Page Layout.

**Standard Fields that are HIDDEN out-of-the-box and are critical:**

At this point, we have only discussed fields that are actually *visible* on the Page Layout for Lead records that come out-of-the-box within Salesforce. There are still Standard fields within the Lead Object in Salesforce (as many other Objects out-of-the-box also have critical Standard hidden fields) that need to be made visible and added to the Page Layout. If your company has been using Salesforce for a while, some of these fields may already be made visible and on the Page Layout. Here is a list of some of the important fields that you do not need to create as Custom fields are as follows:

**Email Opt Out** – a specific record has Opted-Out of receiving emails.

**Do Not Call** – a specific record has requested to not be called.

**Fax Opt-Out** – a specific record has requested to not be faxed. Yes, this is still a thing and is actually more common than you think.

**Description** – a very large free text field that allows your users to add a description about the record.

**Fax** – a Fax number.

None of the above fields need to be customized, they simply need to be made visible and added to the page layout for users to then be able to have access to these fields and update them when necessary. Please note, there are other standard fields that are hidden, and you can view all of them by going through the back end of Salesforce.

Now that we have discussed Standard fields that come out-of-the-box with Salesforce, next comes the critical part in compiling the relevant custom fields you need to create within the system for users to have access to and populate accordingly. As stated prior, one of the easiest ways to start this process is to role play and ask your team questions to create an open-ended discussion. An example of this role play that is specific to the Lead Object is the following:

1. Walk me through the current process if I were to give you a brand new lead. In essence, what would you do first? You may get the traditional answer like, I call them, or email them or something else. Again, this is going to be an open-ended discussion and your personnel may sometimes be jumping around or skipping steps. It is up to you to bring all participants back to the question at hand, especially if some personnel goes off on tangents. Keep your discussions relevant to the specific part of the process being documented.
2. If you received a basic response or got off topic for a bit, then you could say something like, "Great, but let's say that you connected with the Lead, either on the phone or they responded to your email, what questions or pieces of information do you ask to help identify this is a potential prospect?" To be clear, what are the "Qualifying Questions" to determine if this is a viable lead that could be converted into an Opportunity (aka sales deal)? Did you see what just happened there? Let's review. Even if your participant was asking various questions or going a bit ahead or off topic, bring the team back to the initial question to discuss the specifics of each step of the processes your user's experience on a daily basis. That very question regarding the "Qualifying Questions" will get your sales team providing a number of critical fields that need to be added into Salesforce. A word of caution: you need to take each field one at a time and define the following:
    a. What is the purpose of this field?
    b. Is this field really important for everyone or does only one person ever ask this question? Maybe everyone should be asking this question if only one person is asking this question, or is this really not relevant? If the field is determined not relevant; it's better off for the user to add it as a related Note or in a free text field that combines other items. *Only add fields that provide value.*
    c. Who is the source of this information? Meaning, which users will

be getting the information from the source and actually updating this field? This then leads to a follow up question of, "Who needs access to this field?" Answering these questions help determine if varying departments need different page layouts to display fields only relevant to them. Some fields are on the Page Layout, but are set to 'read only' because those specific users may not be the source of the information, but still need to see the information. Other departments may not need to see this field(s) at all and can be removed from their Page Layout.

d. Continue to ask, what else? What other Qualifying Questions or critical information do you want to track? If you keep asking, people will keep thinking. Sometimes it is recommended after compiling all the business requirements, to get on an actual initial sales call with a team member to see if there was any other information that you hear from the prospect or your user asks, that was not mentioned during your meeting. Getting all the qualifying questions is key in ensuring an effective Salesforce Implementation takes place, as this information will assist the company in gaining system adoption due to the value the system is providing its users.

e. After you compile your qualifying questions, the next step specific to the Lead Object is as follows:

   i. **Custom Company Fields:** Is there any information about the company that is critical to your business? Qualifying Questions were great to identify if the Lead is valid and if they are interested in your products/services. But, you may also want to have company specific fields that may be relevant to your business. For example, a medical device company may want to know how many medical beds does the hospital have in total? This may be a numerical value field, or it may be a set picklist value range. Either way, if this Lead becomes 'Qualified' and is converted to proceed to an Opportunity, this '# of Beds' field information will be mapped over onto the newly created Account Record. Be sure to talk through any fields that may be relevant to capture about the company itself to help gauge a company's fit with your organization and product/service offerings.

   ii. **Social Media:** Track any Social Media about the individual lead record.

iii. **Unqualified Reason:** Determine the reasons as why Leads can be unqualified, so your sales personnel can document the reason and also provide context regarding what had taken place. The potential unqualified reason can help your Marketing Department build specific campaigns that could help re-engage those types of specific Leads.

iv. **Additional Contact Information:** You may need to add custom fields to capture more contact information, as the Standard Phone, Mobile, Fax and Email fields may not be enough. Just be sure to keep the naming conventions very specific regarding the additional contact information fields, so users populate the information correctly.

Let's do a quick review of the process to identify fields for a Standard Object. You started off by first reviewing the Standard fields and determined which fields are applicable, and which are not to your company. Some of the Standard fields that are applicable can be customized based on their field type and needs to be updated to display relevant information that is applicable to your company. You also reviewed the hidden fields, to ensure you are using any and all applicable Standard fields first. The next step is to then walk through and discuss possible custom fields to ensure you are capturing all the specific data points relevant to the Object you are reviewing with your team. This process is a great way to make sure no fields have been forgotten about and to be sure only relevant data points are going to be captured.

# Step 6: Optional Salesforce Features Per Object

NOW THAT YOU HAVE ALL of the Fields compiled, the next step is to go through what optional items are needed to complete the Object's business requirements prior to any automation discussions. These items are broken out as follows:

**Need for Record Types?**

Are there any Record Types that are applicable for this Object? In essence, are there different types of records that can be created that have different processes and/or varying fields displayed depending on the type of record being created? If the answer to any of the above items is 'Yes', then most likely you will need to create Record Types for that specific Object. Please note, if there is only 1 field or a very small number of fields that cause the different Record Types needed, then most likely it is not necessary to create Record Types for that object (an example of an exception to this rule is if you have different sales processes on the Opportunity Object for each specific type of sale at your company).

Typically, Record Types are used to be able to capture the variations of the types of records you may need to create and only display fields that are relevant to each specific type of record created. An easy example of a use case for Record Types is creating 'Wholesale' Accounts and 'Retail' Accounts. Wholesale will maybe have the standard Industry field on their page layout and a few other fields such as a 'Frequency of Purchase' field and 'Areas Serviced' field as examples. But on the 'Retail' Account page layout none of those fields are applicable, and instead having demographic fields for marketing purposes is more relevant for users to reference and populate. Both use the Account Object, but the Object can be tailored for you to track different types of records that have relevant processes and data points displayed on their page layouts through the use of Record Types.

**How Many Page Layouts?**

Regardless if you use Record Types or not, you still need to customize at least one Page Layout per Object. What is optional is to determine if you need to create multiple page layouts for the same Object. A simple way of doing Page Layouts is to create one Page Layout that everyone uses, or you can create multiple Page Layouts. With multiple Page Layouts, each Page Layout is assigned to a Profile and those users then only see the information that is displayed per the Page Layout you create for them.

This way, you are making users page display data points that are relevant to their position and streamlines their day-to-day items. The choice is yours to use one Page Layout or make multiple Page Layouts, as both strategies can be used and is decided based on a per Object basis and what users need to have access to. Please keep in mind that the goal overall is to make the system efficient and effective, and a great way of accomplishing this is only displaying what is needed to the corresponding user's position at the company. If you use Record Types, you can create a page layout per Record Type (just like you can create one Page Layout for all to reference except this is per record type) or you can create multiple Page Layouts per Record Type that is assigned per Profile, which are assigned to each specific user. Again, this is all based on the Object you are customizing and if multiple Page Layouts need to be created per Profile and if Record Types are being utilized for this Object, will assist in determining if additional varying Page Layouts are necessary.

**Need for a Custom Object?**

You first need to understand what a Custom Object actually is. A Custom Object is an Object that does not come out-of-the-box in Salesforce. You create a Custom Object to capture additional information, that is related to the starting Object of identifying that you need to capture more information regarding. For example, a school may have their Student Records in Salesforce under Accounts (most likely as a Person Account), but they also need to track the Classes in which the students have completed, registered for next year, and are currently enrolled in. This 'Classes' Object is very specific to the schooling world and does not come out-of-the-box when a school (or anyone) purchases Salesforce, and therefore, the need for a Custom Object has now been determined. This way, when a school counselor pulls up the student's record within Salesforce, the counselor sees all the general contact information, the year the student started at the school, etc., on their main Account record. Related to the student's Account record are a number of Objects that are Standard (like Activities logged, Opportunities for billing) and Custom Objects, like the Classes Object (that we determined needed to be created), in order for the Counselor to see all the pertinent information to do their job function from the main student Account record. A Custom Object is the same thing as a Standard Object, except you create them within your Salesforce as they are specific only to your company to collect additional information. Whether you are reviewing a Standard Object or already discussing a Custom Object, determining if additional information needs to be captured that is related to the initial Object you are reviewing, is a critical juncture of compiling your Business Requirements.

**Custom Objects are valuable for the following reasons:**

- **Parse out fields/data:** To not have numerous custom fields on a single Object, it may be best to parse out this data captured through a Custom Object. In essence, you can create a Custom Object that may only have a one-to-one relationship. A common example for this is a 'Project' Object for project management and is best to parse out this data into two separate objects (Opportunity Object and the Project Object) for user efficiency purposes and data relevance by Object.
- **Need to create multiple records (one-to-many relationship):** Multiple records need to be created on this Custom Object and each record can be associated with one central record. Like in our Student example above, imagine creating a field per class that a University offers and then having status fields per class all mixed with the student contact data and other data points! That would be impractical and instead, you can create a Custom Object so Users can create multiple records that relate to the initial Object (in this example was the Student Account Record) that represents each Class record and the relevant data per Class accordingly.
- **Use as a reference:** This is a less common use case for a simple Salesforce Implementation, but still is great to know and very effective for various reasons. These Custom Objects may or may not be related to any other Object(s). An example is to have a Custom Object as a reference that may include information that can be included within a calculation on the other Object record you are on or to pull information from a field(s) from the reference Object record to populate back to the main Object record. In any case, you can create a Custom Object and records within the Custom Object to have specific information populated via fields, that can be related or not related to anything, and with added automation, can be used to interact with other Objects/Records within your Salesforce. In essence, these Custom Objects are used as a 'table reference'.

# Step 7: Automation Needs

AUTOMATION NEEDS: THIS EXERCISE IS best to review and identify once the custom objects, fields, page layouts, and record types have all been implemented. This way you can visualize all of the fields and the page layout(s) in a clean and clear manner to determine if automation is necessary. Many personnel may say they want something automated when compiling field requirements initially, but when they actually see a live version of the fields and Object customizations in place, they may deem the prior requested automation no longer necessary. Therefore, automation is better left until after all other items that were discussed are complete.

**Are Workflows Needed?**

Workflows are point-and-click to create, including the criteria (unless you build a formula based criteria that requires formula syntax) and the functionality itself of the items listed below. Just know with workflows, as simple as they are to quickly setup and create, they do have limitations in the flexibility of their capabilities, and you will run into these limitations based on a business requirement that will cause you to choose an alternative Salesforce automation feature instead. *Think of Workflows to take care of automated items that are Object specific and that target records based on specific criteria, to then create a task, send an email alert and/or do simple field updates.*

**Step 1:** Choose the Object - When creating a Workflow, you first determine the Object in which you would like to create the Workflow on.

**Step 2:** Workflow Kick Off - Then you determine at what point you want the Workflow to kick off based on when a record is created, edited and/or when a record is updated that then meets the specific criteria for the workflow to be initiated. Please note, just because a Workflow is initiated, DOES NOT mean that it will actually then do something. The next step after this is when the Workflow evaluates specific criteria you set, for the Workflow to be able to proceed or not with an action. Workflow kick off options are the following:

*Created:* If this option is chosen, then this Workflow kicks off only when a new record is created and will never be evaluated again going forward. An example to use this is when a new Lead record is created, and you would like to auto-create a 'Welcome Task' for the Lead Owner to follow up with this lead in 2 days' time from the created date. In this case, you would want this new task auto-created each time a new Lead record is created and never again.

*Created, and every time it's edited:* A Workflow will always be evaluated with any record creation or edit. This Workflow option is kicked off every time a record is created and edited. An example of this use case is if you have a 'Field Update' you want every time to run to ensure the calculation is correct and taking into any and all changes without having to specify specific changes.

*Created: and any time it's edited to subsequently meet criteria:* A Workflow will be evaluated only if the criteria was met from initial creation of the record or after the record is saved and updated to then meet specific criteria. This way, if a record prior to editing had already met the criteria, this Workflow will then not be kicked off again as it has already met the criteria. It is only when something was updated or initially created (if the record prior had not met the criteria specified) will then kick off the Workflow. An example of this is if you want to date stamp a custom date field called "Working Date Stamp" with the date when a user changes the status field of a Work Order Object Record from "New" to "Working". In this example, a specific field that was set to a specific picklist option (user changed the status field to "Working") would be the criteria and only when this is met would this type of Workflow then kick off and be chosen for the type of Workflow you are building.

**Step 3:** Input Criteria to target specific records: Once you identify when you want the Workflow to kick off, the next step is to input the actual specific criteria you want to filter down to target which record is to be included in the final actions of the workflow.

**Quick Review of Steps 1 – 3 within this Workflow section:** You first identified which Object you want to automate. Then you decided when you want the Workflow to be kicked off based on your business requirements. Lastly, you input the criteria to filter down and target the specific record(s) you would like to proceed to the final actions.

**Step 4:** Determine the outcome of the Workflow by understanding each of the final actions capabilities which are the following:

*Task Creation:* Are there any Tasks that need to be auto created? These may be based on a status or stage change of a record. Maybe when a field is populated or set to a specific value to be reminded to do something next. Or maybe a time-based task that is created based on the amount of time that has passed.

*Field Update:* If a user (or something else like an Integration with an external system) populates a field, or a combination of multiple field criteria, then do other fields need to be populated with a specific value or information?

*Email Alert:* Similar to the Task creation, based on a change or update or creating a new record, does an email alert need to be sent to outside vendors or prospects/customers or to internal personnel? Email Alerts can also be time-dependent so you can set the date based on a number of days that have passed or prior to a date to initiate an email alert.

*Send an Outbound Message:* This is the last Workflow capability that we will not go into details regarding as the above actions are simple steps to fulfill basic automated needs.

**Helpful Hint:** Some workflows have only one action or you can create a number of actions that are a mix of each type as you may want multiple items to happen. An example is to create an Email Alert and also do a field update as final actions for a specific Workflow.

### Is a Process Builder Needed?

Process Builder is a great next step to use as a Salesforce automation feature if you determined that a Workflow will be too limited in what you are trying to accomplish. First, the term "Process Builder" may sound intimidating but have no fear, as this feature is also a point-and-click feature and does not require any code to build. It follows a very similar process to what was described within the "Workflow" section above. Just like Workflows, you may have to write formula syntax for criteria build, or specifying the criteria of what types of record you are filtering down to if you are not able to use the point-and-click criteria option. Having to write a formula syntax may also apply if you are using the field update feature (to simply update a field) in the Process Builder to calculate a formula or to pull through data from a related object/record. Again, this is a point-and-click feature and can accomplish a number of automation items simply utilizing point-and-click throughout the entire Process Builder. Lastly, think of the Process Builder as a number of If/Then statements to determine, if this (criteria) then what automation(s) should take place.

- Process Builder includes the Workflow capabilities of Email Alerts, Task Creation and Field Updates. The Process Builder even takes these options a step further because it has the flexibility to reference related Objects to be able to update various fields or send alerts based on more criteria options. At this point, you might be thinking, "If this feature does nearly all the features of what a Workflow can do, then why not just use Process Builder?" The answer is yes, you can, but again, Workflows are simplistic to build and is a very useful feature to use for those basic automation needs that is Object specific.
- Process Builder has a number of additional capabilities, such as the ability to

update Related Records or even create a Related Record, which is something that a Workflow is not able to do.

- In addition, Process Builder is able to be used with other automation features, such as:
  - o Start/invoke other custom code
  - o Launch a Flow (discussed later in this book)
  - o Auto-submit for an Approval Process (also discussed later in this book)
  - o And other items that are not as common but still available to fulfill a number of automation needs
- One reason why people like Process Builder is because you can have a number of these If/Then statements and capabilities happening in an order you choose and are displayed in a full-screen decision tree. This allows you to clearly see within a Process Builder, all the steps available and the outcome per step in a single view for that one Object. In essence, if a record enters the Process Builder because it was kicked off by a certain action, then the record enters the first step, and the Process Builder determines if the criteria for that step you created is met. If the criteria is met, then the record proceeds, otherwise the record goes to the second step, and so on. The record can even enter into a number of steps as it may hit multiple varying criteria. It is a simple decision tree with either a Yes or No and then the record moves to the next item or it stops on a specific step you deem within the decision tree. You have the full point-and-click capability to either have a record only go through a specific step or go in order through each step you desire to ensure the outcome(s) is what you want to happen as a final action.
- Lastly, Process Builder does have limitations of what it can accomplish and its capabilities through this point-and-click feature and when you hit those limits, then it is most likely the time to look at another automation feature, such as 'Flows'.

## Is a Flow Needed?

Before creating a Flow, it is recommended to review the prior automation capabilities as we discussed above, to see if they can fulfill your business requirements. Flows are an automation feature that is a step above the Process Builder and near the top of automation features that are provided within Salesforce that is point-and-click based, without having to write custom code like "Apex".

To identify if a Flow is needed, you could ask yourself the following sample questions:

- *Step-By-Step Guide:* Does there need to be a guided Step-By-Step Process for users to populate various fields that everyone should follow on a consistent basis? If yes, then this is a great capability to assist in a guidance process or by displaying specific data fields on a user's screen to go through each screen element until the Flow has successfully completed. You can have the guidance process be dynamic, which means based on the information the User populates, can then dictate the next screen and what happens next.

- *Create/Update/Get/Delete Record and Logic:* Do you need an automated process to create/update/assign/identify new or existing records with potential logic rules and a multi-layer decision tree? You can use this feature in a number of ways and can even use multiple Flow features all within the same Flow. For example, with the example of the step-by-step guide above; let's say the user is a receptionist and prior to picking up the phone, she starts the 'Caller Lookup Flow' from within Salesforce (assuming the company does not have a CTI aka Phone integration into their Salesforce). The receptionist can first greet the individual caller and then asks for a unique identifier from the person calling (in this Flow example, the caller's email address will be used as the unique identifier). Once the email address is inputted, the User can click the next button and the Flow can have logic implemented to 'Get Records' (a simple way of phrasing this is to look up existing records within the system) to see if there is a matching record. If a match exists, then the Flow will bring up the caller's Salesforce record and the Receptionist will be able to review the caller's information and proceed to the next step. If the record does not exist, the Flow then brings the receptionist to a different screen that allows the Receptionist to input the required information to create a new record and proceed to the next step. Did you notice that logic can be built to identify a match through 'Get Records' and then depending on the logic to determine the next screen and what happens next? Flows can be built to fulfill a number of processes through a guided process, so your users do not make a mistake on what information is needed, and not forget to ask the right questions and what to do next.
- Flows can be used in a number of ways and the capabilities of having Elements through drag and drop "Data Items", such as Create/Update Records, or "Logic items" that could follow a decision tree that you create and "Interactions" that are specific actions or screen base displays; these are all features available to be dragged and dropped onto a canvas and follow the steps that you dictate per item. From start to finish, each Flow

uses a combination of these 'Elements' to complete the entire process in the most efficient manner based on the decisions that resulted through to the end.

- One of the most important items to know regarding Flows is that you can reference or utilize Objects that are not actually related to other Objects. This is very similar to what we discussed in determining the need for a Custom Object that can be used as a 'Reference Table'. Even though the Custom Object is not related to any other Object, you can use automation, such as a Flow, to reference and use the information on these records to then do something else. For example, you can do a calculation and use a field from a specific matching record from this Custom Object being used as a 'Reference Table', to then pull that field and insert the value as a variable input as part of an overall calculation.
- The way a Flow can be kicked off is through either a manual process (user clicking on a button), or can be scheduled, record triggered (a record edit or creation) and a few other options. The flexibility of when something happens is a valuable capability provided with this point-and-click feature.

**Helpful Hint:** Flows are the future of Salesforce's point-and-click automation and eventually will include nearly all (if not all) 'Workflow' and 'Process Builder' capabilities that were previously discussed, in addition to a number of other features. It appears that 'Workflows' and 'Process Builder' could be retired at some point and that Flows will be the main feature to add point-and-click automations into Salesforce.

## Is Apex Needed?

Lastly, is the infamous 'Apex' that people either have no idea what you are talking about, have somewhat of an idea, feel comfortable with 'Apex' or are true experts in coding with 'Apex'. It does not matter whichever level you are, because now after reading this book, you are at least in the somewhat of an idea range. 'Apex' is simply the custom code language that is used to automate or do nearly anything within the Salesforce platform that you code it to do. Apex is broken down into "Classes" and "Triggers". Think of "Classes" as a grouping of a number of "Triggers" and these "Triggers" are specific coded actions to fulfill various business requirements. It is typical (and most likely optimal) to have one "Class" per Object that calls on multiple "Triggers" per Object that all rollup to this one "Class". This just makes the system run more efficiently and keeps things tidy within your Salesforce.

- When you are compiling your business requirements and determine that an automation requested can only be accomplished through 'Apex', it is important to specify the exact process you want to take place and work through all the if/then items and most importantly, the 'exceptions to the rule'. Anyone writing the 'Apex' code will need a step-by-step process of what you are wanting to accomplish and all the criteria of what to include and what to exclude. This will help your developer to refine the criteria accordingly as it may be easier to include the exceptions, versus what is to be included.

Double check the following:

- Be sure you cannot accomplish this through a Workflow, Process Builder or Flow.
- Be sure your process is as close to final as possible because changes could then cause the custom code needing to be updated to follow the new process.
- Be sure to document all the details of what has to happen prior to the Apex code being initiated and kicks off.
- Be sure to document all the exceptions or records excluded, so you know that you are not missing any additional exceptions that you may have forgotten. It also may give you ideas to add anything else to the prior bullet point of what needs to happen, or information needed to be populated, prior to the 'Trigger' being initiated.

Having all this documented allows you or your developer to decide the number of 'Triggers' needed. In addition, having the requirements thoroughly documented is valuable in case you or your developer have any other questions prior to starting. Items may come up during the coding process for clarification purposes or changes that may need to be made to the process, which is normal, as there may have been items not discussed or forgotten about, that may need to be answered in order to finalize the custom code.

**Helpful Hint:** Custom Code cannot be written directly into the Production version of your Salesforce. Custom Code must be written in a Sandbox. In addition, this also allows your users to test the custom code within the Sandbox to ensure everything is working correctly. Once the custom code is approved by your test users, then you or your developer will then create a Test Class to ensure the custom code fulfills the Salesforce platform requirements, before being able to be deployed into the live Production instance to be used by your Salesforce users.

## *Other Key Features:*

### Validation Rules Needed?

Validation Rules are formula syntax only (meaning you have to know how to build formulas that follow syntax requirements) that you can implement for optimal data integrity and making sure things are populated correctly. Some common use cases are the following:

- How data is inputted in a specific field. For example, not allowing any letters within a numbers field when tracking 'No. of Employees'.

- Requiring users to populate various fields if another field is to be populated or populated with a specific value. For example, a user updates a Lead Status to "Unqualified" and selects the reason for the qualification as 'Bad Contact Information', but you may still want them to populate an unqualified reason description field as well. Therefore, the user will be prompted to provide additional details within the unqualified reason description field.
- Requiring users to populate fields prior to allowing the user to update the status or stage of a record. For example, certain fields have to be populated on the Opportunity record at a specific stage, prior to the user being able to progress the Opportunity to the next sales stage within the sales process.
- There are a number of use cases that can be used for Validation Rules, but just know, the core functionality is to ensure data integrity or that information is populated correctly.

### Approval Process Needed?

Is there an Approval Process that is required for one of your specific business requirements? If so, what is the status, stage, or a mix of criteria when a record needs to be submitted for an approval? A common Approval process can be used for approving a Quote Record within Salesforce that needs to be reviewed and approved by a manager, prior to sending off a quote to a prospect/customer for their review. You can use Approvals for any Object for items that need to be approved. For example, if you have Accounting integrated or part of your Salesforce Instance, some people want to have an Approval Process to review Billing records prior to being remitted to a customer. Another example is a Project Requirements Record as a Custom Object within your Salesforce, which needs to be approved for all the tasks assigned prior to scheduling a kick-off with your customer. The standard Approval Process within Salesforce is point-and-click, and it actually guides you step-by-step per each Approval Process step. For example, it identifies who needs to approve the record, which can be designated to a specific user(s) and/or can be dynamic based on a custom field or Approving Manager designation. Then you have the choice of what happens when the Record is Approved or Rejected. In essence, you have the ability to add point-and-click customizations that are near exact to Workflow Capabilities as outlined prior. Such as, sending an email notification to the person who submitted the record and that the Record was not approved. Or create a Task for the record owner within Salesforce as part of the 'Rejection' step items if the record is not Approved. You can also do 'Field Updates' (most likely you would want to update the Stage or Status field or other fields) to a Not Approved status/stage. Lastly, you can provide a detailed reason for not approving the record. This way, your user who submitted the record or any other users you designate, can receive an email notification and/or task and review the reasoning for the not approved record to make the appropriate changes to re-submit the record, if your Approval Process permits doing so. Of course, you would create each of these steps within the Approval Process, so each user knows what they need to do next to proceed accordingly with the use of Approval Process automation (near exact to Workflow Capabilities). Approval processes are very effective when it is truly necessary to get a second set of eyes on information prior to providing something forward-facing to prospects/customers or allowing users to proceed to the next step of the process.

**Helpful Hints When Compiling Business Requirements for an Approval Process:**

- Be sure to determine if an Approval is always required, or if there are exceptions of when an Approval is not necessary. If there are exceptions, document both the criteria that is required and the exceptions, as you are able to configure the Approval Process to allow users to bypass the Approval Process when it is not necessary to obtain an approval. A simple way to achieve this is to use an automation feature prior to the Approval Process (like a Process Builder) to determine if an Approval is needed or to kick off the Approval process.
- Be very clear in the criteria and at what status/stage or specific point within the process on a record of when the Approval Process needs to start.
- Document who the approvers are, and if multiple approvers are required versus only one.
- If the Approving person(s) are out of town or out of the office for any reason, be sure to include alternative Approvers within your process, so there are no delays in obtaining an approval.
- Be sure to discuss the entire process, for every single scenario, to ensure the automation (such as Field Updates, Notifications via email and/or Tasks and others) are working at each juncture of the Approval Process. For example, if your Approval Process requires two Approvers and the initial Approver approves the record and the second Approver does not, be sure to designate and test that the correct users are being notified and the information being captured on the record and per field is being updated accordingly.
- Finally, Approval Processes can be initiated by either having the user manually click a button to 'Submit for Approval' and/or automated through a Process Builder or other automation tools that can be used in conjunction with this automation capability.

## Is a Visualforce Page Needed?

A Visualforce Page is a custom-coded page that can display data and/or various other Object Records onto a single page, based on your specifications. A Visualforce Page can have standard or custom buttons displayed on the Page as well, so users can then perform an action or initiate an Apex Trigger, to then do something else. This feature allows you the flexibility to display a number of records and data points you think are best for your users to interact with or need information to reference in a consolidated page.

*Examples that may cause you to need a Visualforce Page are the following:*

In some cases, you may not be able to use the standard Page Layout configuration for a specific Object to display all the pertinent details that your users are requesting to have visible within one page. This typically happens when your users need additional information displayed that is located on other 'indirect' related Objects, but want to be able to see these 'indirect' related Object's records on a single page. For example, the Case Object is directly related to the Account Object and when a User is reviewing a specific Account record, can then easily see all the related Case records associated with that Account record with the use of the standard Page Layout configuration. But if your users wanted to also see all the Case Comments per each Case record without having to click into each Case record from the Account record page would require a Visualforce Page. The 'indirect' related Object in this example is the Case Comments, because even though Case Comments are directly related to the Case Object, and the Case Object, in turn, is directly related to the Account Object, still does not permit the User to see all the Case Comments from the Account level and would require a Visualforce Page to display this 'indirect' related Object.

Furthermore, you can also create a Visualforce page to run an automation (like update or create records) behind the scenes. For example, your team may want to be able to select each product line offering that will then create an Opportunity per product line in mass, that is related to the starting Account record, all within a single page. Currently, out-of-the-box with Salesforce, you would need a user to create each Opportunity one at a time manually without any automation added to your Salesforce. But with the use of Salesforce functionality the system provides, such as a Visualforce Page, you can create a custom button called "Multiple Product Opportunities", where a user can click on this button and be directed to a custom Visualforce Page, that displays each Product Line, and the user can select which are applicable and update the price accordingly. They can then click a button called "Finish" on the Visualforce Page and it could tell them something like the number of

Opportunities that were successfully created, while in the background it actually creates each of the Opportunity records related to the Account in mass per product line with the pricing inputted by the user. In essence, you can code a custom page in which your users are able to create multiple opportunities, all at once and per product line. Talk about time efficiency! This is just one example of the power of a Visualforce Page that can be created to run a number of automated items.

Other examples of needing a Visualforce Page include rendering a document, such as a Customer Statement, or you purchased an App on the Salesforce AppExchange and some of the App functionality has Visualforce Components that need to be added to the Object Page Layout for users to access the App capabilities.

Again, Visualforce Pages allow the flexibility for you to code a Page that can display fields/various records/buttons to make it easier to either display information to your Users and/or execute custom code to automate an action or process.

## Step 8: Salesforce AppExchange

IT IS HIGHLY RECOMMENDED THAT you look at the AppExchange for all the Apps that are pre-developed for the Salesforce Platform. If you think of something you are looking to add into your Salesforce and do not want to build it from scratch, then the AppExchange is a great resource to purchase (sometimes Apps are free) a pre-developed program that you customize to your company's needs. This is a very simple way to extend your Salesforce capabilities and to then just tailor the app to your company specifics. The same process of compiling your business requirements that you have read in this book applies to any purchased Apps, as they will have their own Objects, Fields, Automation etc., pre-built and it is up to you to decide what is necessary to ensure you compile all the business requirements to continuously be successful on the Salesforce Platform!

## Step 9: Consulting Partners

IT IS IDEAL TO HIRE experts regarding Salesforce customizations that can implement the business requirements you and team have now compiled. Our recommended Consulting Partners that specialize in Salesforce Implementations, Salesforce Customizations, Salesforce Training and Salesforce Monthly Management can be requested directly through our website on the Contact Us page.

Made in the USA
Coppell, TX
09 February 2024

28802164R00025